DOUGLASS AND LISA-MARIE
HATCHER

W$N WITH DECENCY

HOW TO USE
YOUR BETTER ANGELS
FOR BETTER BUSINESS

We're reaching a point in human history, where we will have to reimagine imagination itself. The boundaries of what the human mind could fathom, even just a few short years ago, are changing and extending. As the landscape shifts, we will need a new cartography and new skills to go with it.

COPYRIGHT PAGE
Copyright 2020 © by communicate4IMPACT

ISBN: 978-1-7344469-0-6 Paperback
ISBN: 978-1-7344469-1-3 eBook

All product and company names are trademarks™ or registered® trademarks of their respective holders. Use of them does not imply any affiliation with or endorsement by them with the exception of the references to the U.K. marketing firm, Atomic, where communicate4IMPACT has an affiliate relationship. In addition, reference to or the use of any trademarks™ or registered® trademarks is solely for illustrative purposes.

Always do right; this will gratify some people and astonish the rest. [1]

—Mark Twain,
Note to the Young People's Society, Greenpoint
Presbyterian Church, 1901

For those who raised us and for those we're raising.

CONTENTS

Preface: Making The Business Case For Decency 1
Introduction: Welcome To The Era Of Obsolescence And The
    Age Of Unknowability. 5
Chapter One: Humility 11
Chapter Two: Empathy 27
Chapter Three: Vulnerability 43
Chapter Four: Gratitude. 57
Chapter Five: Generosity 75
Chapter Six: Keep the Human in Human Enterprise 87
About the Authors 89
Endnotes 91

PREFACE

MAKING THE BUSINESS CASE FOR DECENCY

This book makes the business case for decency. It's the kind of decency that for many companies has proven to yield dividends—dividends that include greater employee retention, increased customer loyalty, higher earnings, more sales, faster innovation, better information-sharing, more streamlined communication, stronger trust, heightened brand awareness, enviable brand reputation, and overall greater growth and scale.

That's a boatload of dividends.

So, while you catch your breath, we'll talk for a minute about how this book was born. *Win With Decency* was inspired by our work in the business storytelling space, where we train business leaders in the art and science of making things matter and moving people to act. In our workshops, we teach that certain human qualities are the beating heart of business storytelling.

Those qualities are humility, empathy, and vulnerability. Humility allows you to put your audience first, empathy puts you in your audience's shoes, and vulnerability creates a connection with your audience. Taken together, these qualities help you humanize your content and make it relatable and actionable. But over the course of teaching our workshops and interacting with our participants, we began to wonder if the qualities of humility, empathy, and vulnerability were unique to business storytelling or if they had other applications for business success.

Looking for answers, we put on our research caps and began to curate content around these three cornerstone qualities of business storytelling. We found success stories and insights shared by captains of industry and thought leaders such as Steve Jobs (founder and former CEO of Apple), Bill Taylor (cofounder of *Fast Company*), Satya Nadella (CEO of Microsoft), Dr. Brené Brown (professor and author), and many others.

Not surprisingly, when examining these stories and insights, we ran across two additional human qualities that had positive applications for business. These two qualities were gratitude and generosity. So, then there were five! Humility, empathy, vulnerability, gratitude and generosity: human qualities that, for us, are foundational for decency. We discovered that these five qualities, often associated with being a better person, are also often associated with business growth, brand differentiation, and competitive advantage.

Now that we had our list of five qualities and supporting business cases, we wanted to tie them together under one theme. We thought about virtuous competition, but that just didn't seem to be a big enough umbrella to cover it. What really seemed to bring everything together was this idea of decency as a business strategy for winning in both the workplace and the marketplace.

And for us, the qualities driving that decency are our better angels. *Win With Decency: How to Use Your Better Angels for Better Business* is a collection of real-world success stories combined with our own insights. We show you how to transform the five human qualities of humility, empathy, vulnerability, gratitude, and generosity into the *Win With Decency* skills you need to lead and succeed in the 2020s and beyond.

INTRODUCTION

WELCOME TO THE ERA OF OBSOLESCENCE AND THE AGE OF UNKNOWABILITY

> *The dogmas of the quiet past are inadequate to the stormy present. The occasion is piled high with difficulty and we must rise with the occasion. As our case is new, we must think anew and act anew.*[2]
>
> **—Abraham Lincoln**

THINGS ARE MOVING so fast you can almost feel the earth shifting beneath your feet. We're at the tail end of a technological wave driven by the internet and digital connectivity. At the same time, we find ourselves on the threshold of the 2020s, where we are on the cusp of a new technological wave—one that will be driven by 5G, the Internet of Things (IoT), Artificial Intelligence (AI), Blockchain, Robotics, various Virtual Realities, 3D Printing, and much more. We're entering a time where if you can dream it, you can create it.

IMAGE SOURCE: Pixabay

Nearly every aspect of how we live, work, and play is poised for dramatic change. Imagine the following: downloading a two-hour HD movie in a matter of seconds; receiving world-class healthcare treatments remotely through robotics; managing supply-chains where errors, inefficiencies, and dangers are immediately flagged and corrected; living in smart cities with less traffic congestion, more efficient energy sources, and yes—in time—driverless cars; and experiencing retail that's immersive, hyper-customized, and predictive.

How we go about our daily lives will undergo massive shifts. The global economy is positioned for change as well. Gross Domestic Product (GDP) projections alone are pretty staggering. One research company forecasts that this wave of new networks and associated technologies could add up to $17 trillion to the global GDP by 2035. That's more than $1 trillion added to the global GDP every year for the next decade and a half.³

So, what does any of this have to do with the *Win With Decency* strategy? Well, one of the cornerstones of our approach is continuous learning. Continuous learning allows you to be both defensive and offensive in a fast-changing future filled with huge unknowns. By defensive, we mean protecting yourself against blind spots and being disrupted. By offensive, we mean being able to anticipate market needs that drive innovation as well as anticipate market shifts before your competitors do. As one of the architects of business management, Peter Drucker, said: "Learning is a lifelong process of keeping abreast of change. And the most pressing task is to teach people how to learn."

Here's why we need to be continuous learners. A century ago, it would have taken thirty-five years for half of what an engineer learned as a student to lose its relevance. By the 1960s, that number had shrunk to ten years.⁴ Today, the half-life of a learned skill is estimated to be five years.⁵ So, what does this mean? It means the value of our skills is depreciating at faster rates. A new skill we learn today is becoming less relevant sooner.

Not only that, the jobs landscape is changing rapidly as well. According to an Oxford University study, nearly half of today's jobs will be eliminated over the next twenty-five years.⁶ Dell Technologies estimates that as much as 85 percent of the jobs that will exist in ten years have not even been invented yet.⁷ All of this begs the question: how can you prepare for a future where the usefulness of a skill begins to depreciate as soon as you learn it? How can you prepare for a job market that doesn't exist?

Welcome to the era of obsolescence and the age of unknowability.

The marketplace is responding to the challenges of obsolescence and unknowability with widespread initiatives to reskill or upskill workforces.

The consulting firm McKinsey conducted a survey of three hundred global executives and found that two-thirds of them rated reskilling or upskilling as a top-10 priority. But here's the problem: only 16 percent of those executives reported feeling "very prepared" to tackle the skills-gap challenge.[8]

And for good reason. The old ways of learning a new skill or upgrading one—while still critical—are no longer enough. Why? Because the old way of teaching was based on "knowns." How do you teach for "unknowns?" It can be quite a head-scratcher and reminds us of something former Defense Secretary Donald Rumsfeld said in a 2002 NATO press conference.

> Now what is the message there? The message is that there are no "knowns." There are things we know that we know. There are known unknowns. That is to say there are things that we now know we don't know. But there are also unknown unknowns. There are things we don't know we don't know. So, when we do the best we can and we pull all this information together, and we then say well that's basically what we see as the situation, that is really only the known knowns and the known unknowns. And each year, we discover a few more of those unknown unknowns. It sounds like a riddle. It isn't a riddle. It is a very serious, important matter.[9]

It's all a little mind-boggling, isn't it? To bridge this preparation gap—to tackle the challenges of skill depreciation and a fast-changing future of unknowns—we offer the *Win With Decency* strategy. In doing so, we share examples of companies and leaders who have transformed one or more of the five named decency qualities into applicable skills, and we want you to benefit from these skills as well.

Here's your roadmap for doing just that. In each chapter, we address one human decency quality and break it down in the following ways: (1) we define the quality; (2) we tie the quality to business storytelling; (3) we make the business case; (4) we show you at least one way you can transform the quality into an applicable skill; and (5) we give you examples of who's using the skill for better business. Our goal is for you to come away prepared with the *Win With Decency* skills you need to gain a competitive advantage and address the unknowns in the coming decade of the 2020s.

Let's get started.

CHAPTER ONE
HUMILITY

Servants focus on others, not themselves. This is true humility: not thinking less of ourselves but thinking of ourselves less.[10]

—**Pastor Rick Warren,**
The Purpose-Driven Life

Define the Quality

WHAT'S THE FIRST thing you think of when you hear the word humility? Modesty, unselfishness, not drawing attention to yourself? Here's a dictionary definition: "the quality or condition of being humble; having a modest opinion or estimate of one's own importance, rank, etc."[11] Fair enough. But how does having a low view of one's own importance write your ticket to business success? Well, it doesn't. So, we're going to think about humility differently.

For our purposes, we'll define humility this way. It comes from *The Purpose-Driven Life* by Pastor Rick Warren: "Servants focus on others, not themselves. This is true humility: not thinking less of ourselves but thinking of ourselves less."[12] When you exercise this definition of humility in your leadership and embed it in your company's culture, you put your customers, consumers, employees, and other stakeholders first—above all else.

Tie It to Business Storytelling

Since this is the first time we'll be tying a quality to business storytelling, let's expand a little more on what business storytelling means. As we said in the preface, business storytelling is the art and science of making things matter and moving people to act.

In today's noisy marketplace, we need business storytelling more than ever to differentiate brands, products, and services. Too often, companies rely on description alone when marketing something. There's a tendency to think that describing something is selling something. But it's not. Description doesn't create meaning. It creates information. Stories create meaning. Apply this thinking when marketing a product or service and you can change your message from being descriptive and static to being relatable and actionable.

Here's an iconic example of what we mean from Steve Jobs. When Jobs launched the iPod in 2001, he could have described it as the latest and greatest MP3 player with more memory and better portability. That would have been an accurate description, right? But instead, Jobs—a master business storyteller—introduced Apple's new product as "a thousand songs in your pocket."[13]

Yes, Jobs described the new product. But he did so in a way that made the product matter. In six words, he made something that was new, relatable—and he ended up writing the headline for nearly every journalist covering the product launch. This is how business storytelling makes things matter and moves people to act.

Now that we've shared an illustration of what we mean by business storytelling, let's tie it back to the quality of humility. When you're sharing a story, humility allows you to shift the focus from yourself to your audience—to meet them where they are, not where you are. Your audience could be your customer, your employees, or other stakeholders. It's anyone you want to influence.

Author Dan Pink demonstrates this concept beautifully in an exercise from his book, *To Sell Is Human*.[14] Here's the exercise for you to try: write an imaginary, uppercase E on your forehead. We'll give you a second… Okay, did you write the E so that others could see it? Or so that you could see it? This is a test of how well you focus on your audience versus yourself.

Keep this exercise in mind the next time you need to build a story around your product or service. Ask yourself, "Who's my audience, and what do I want them to do?" Let the E exercise work its magic.

Make the Business Case

As promised, we'll make the business case for the quality of humility in the workplace. To do that, we'll lean on a study about humility and job performance published by The Foster School of Business at The University of Washington.

The study is entitled, *Expressed Humility in Organizations: Implications for Performance, Teams, and Leadership*.[15]

The study examined the impact of humility on things like job performance, job satisfaction, willingness to learn, engagement with colleagues, and workforce turnover. In this study, the research team defined expressed humility as having three components: *self-awareness, appreciation of others, and teachability.*

Let's look at the first component of expressed humility: *self-awareness*. What are the benefits of self-awareness as a businessperson or leader? Self-awareness enables you to introspectively evaluate your own strengths and weaknesses, which in turn allows you to see yourself more accurately. Believe it or not, one of the founding fathers of modern economics—Adam Smith—had a similar thought when he said, "Behave as if an impartial spectator is watching you. Use the idea of an impartial spectator to step outside yourself and see yourself as others see you."[16]

So, what can be drawn from both the expressed humility study and Adam Smith? It's this: when you have a more accurate view of yourself, you have a better sense of your abilities and are better able to plan your time and efforts to meet performance expectations. Paul Polman, former Unilever CEO, captured this first component of expressed humility well when he said, "Working together on solving something requires a high level of humility and a high level of self-awareness."[17]

Let's look at the flip side of this concept. What happens to job performance if we *don't* practice humility in the form of self-awareness? Well, this is what happens. We risk overestimating our abilities, which can result in insufficient effort, missed deadlines, and lower quality of work—all of which can add up to decreased performance.

One New York firm, Human Ventures, which backs and builds consumer technology companies, believes self-awareness is so critical to leadership, it's developed something called the "self-awareness accelerator," which is conducted for clients by principal and entrepreneur coach, Peter Shallard. As Shallard noted in a *Fast Company* piece: "The number one thing that destroys early-stage, fast-growth companies is hubris, cognitive biases, and blind spots."[18]

The second component of expressed humility involves appreciating the strengths of others. The *Expressed Humility in Organizations* study says that "people who have humility and appreciate others are less likely to discount or devalue the strengths or high performance of those around them. And not only that, they're more likely to model the positive strengths of high performers."[19]

If you're like us, you've probably worked with people who fall on either side of this coin. Most of us, however, would likely agree that working with those who have enough humility to appreciate others' strengths can make a difference—a difference in performance, productivity, and culture. It's these kinds of positive outcomes that add up to what we see as a *decency difference*.

The last component of expressed humility is teachability. Teachability is associated with an openness to feedback and to learning. Humble individuals are more likely to learn from their mistakes and take corrective action after low performance. Teachability that emanates from expressed humility is a must-have trait in a world where skills are depreciating in value as soon as they're learned. If we are to be continuous learners, we must be humble; we must be teachable.

So far, we've talked about the three components of expressed humility and how humility relates to things like job performance. But the impact of humility stands to be much greater in a 2020s economy characterized by exponential change.

Let's look at some potential impacts of self-awareness and teachability. Expressed humility via self-awareness equips us with the mindset we need as business leaders to stop, think, and probe. Humility asks, what have we overlooked? What angles have we not explored? What biases have we not recognized? What opinions should be at the table to challenge and round out our thinking? By the way, humility-inspired questions, like these, aren't meant to be stall tactics. Instead, they're meant to foster the positive paranoia you need to look around corners and recognize blind spots before your competition does. In this sense, humility is a fundamental antidote to disruption.

Eric Schmidt, former Google CEO, once said, "We run this company on questions, not answers." Given that Google is a search engine, that statement was particularly apt. But it also speaks to the power of humility in the *Win With Decency* mindset.

Expressed humility via teachability whets your appetite for knowledge, inspiring you to seek out smarter people and the ideas that come with them. Where others might be threatened by smarter partners, colleagues, or direct reports, humble leaders proactively surround themselves with the best and the brightest. Echoing our definition of humility from Pastor Rick Warren, humble leaders think of themselves less and think more of their organization's shared goals.

Up to this point, we've talked about humility as it relates to things like job performance. But would you believe there is some evidence that humility at the CEO level can help a company's market performance as well? A recent *Wall Street Journal* article talks about just that, citing a study published in the *Strategic Management Journal*.[20] The study found that companies with more humble CEOs have better market performance because they benefit from what the study calls "an expectation discount" in the market.

Researchers discovered that—all things being equal—financial analysts announce lower earnings expectations for companies with more humble CEOs. Setting lower expectations helps companies meet or beat analysts' expectations, which translates into better market performance for companies.[21] Who knew?

There is a strategic value to humility when applied as a skill. It's the very thing that offers us the chance to learn and to grow, to anticipate and to win. That's why we love what Microsoft CEO Satya Nadella has said: "It's time to move from being know-it-alls to learn-it-alls." [22]

The converse is also true—without humility, you limit your awareness of new things. You risk becoming redundant—as Padmasree Warrior, former Cisco Chief Technology Officer, has pointed out. It's a redundancy born out of doing the same thing in the same way as everybody else.[23] Humility taps us on the shoulders and reminds us that it's hard to see the future with blinders on.

Transform the Quality into an Applicable Skill

We've defined humility. We've tied it to business storytelling. We've made the business case. Now, we'll show you how to transform the quality of humility into an applicable skill. One of the easiest things you can do to build humility as a skill is to learn something new, to be a beginner.

Think of something you've always wanted to do, but for whatever reason haven't gotten around to. It could be learning a new language or perhaps a musical instrument. For Steve Jobs, the something new was calligraphy. To give you a concrete example of what we mean, check out this excerpt from his iconic commencement address at Stanford:[24]

> Reed College at that time offered perhaps the best calligraphy instruction in the country. Throughout the campus, every poster, every label on every drawer, was beautifully hand calligraphed. Because I had dropped out and didn't have to take the normal classes, I decided to take a calligraphy class to learn how to do this. I learned about serif and sans serif typefaces, about varying the amount of space between different letter combinations, about what makes great typography great. It was beautiful, historical, artistically subtle in a way that science can't capture, and I found it fascinating.
>
> None of this had even a hope of any practical application in my life. But 10 years later, when we were designing the first Macintosh computer, it all came back to me. And we designed it all into the Mac. It was the first computer with beautiful typography.
>
> If I had never dropped in on that single course in college, the Mac would have never had multiple typefaces or proportionally spaced fonts. And since Windows

just copied the Mac, it's likely that no personal computer would have them. If I had never dropped out, I would have never dropped in on this calligraphy class, and personal computers might not have the wonderful typography that they do.

Of course, it was impossible to connect the dots looking forward when I was in college. But it was very, very clear looking backward ten years later.

Again, you can't connect the dots looking forward; you can only connect them looking backward. So, you have to trust that the dots will somehow connect in your future.

Wow, what a story from what has become one of the great commencement addresses of our time. Now, let's fast forward to a more recent example of someone learning something new—tennis great Serena Williams.

Just as learning about calligraphy had no immediate, practical pertinence to Steve Jobs' life at the time, Serena Williams' calligraphy equivalent doesn't apply to tennis. Her "calligraphy class" is learning to code—as it applies to her fashion line business.[25]

In a world that will increasingly compete on imagination in order to innovate and drive new thinking,[26] finding your "calligraphy class" is not a nice-to-do elective but rather a must-do prerequisite for competitive advantage. If you're a financial analyst whose first love was marine biology, take that first step to rekindle that passion and take some scuba lessons! If you're a doctor whose passion is baking, take a cake-decorating class.

Whatever you choose to try, you will be taking the step of converting the quality of humility into a skill. You will be putting yourself in the state of being a continuous learner; you will be a beginner. And one day in your career, like Steve Jobs, you'll most likely be able to connect the dots looking backwards.

Your homework is to write down three things you've always wanted to do, then pick one and try it out. You don't have to become an expert at it. You don't even have to be proficient at it. The key is to exercise your humility muscles by learning something new. So, what's your calligraphy class going to be?

Now that you are on your way to becoming a beginner at something, why don't you also take a moment to assess your current capacity for humility? Wouldn't you like to know? Since you probably don't want to ask your family or friends to rate your humility quotient, we'll offer this private and quick quiz. It's an assessment tool from a company called Hogan Assessment Systems.

HUMILITY ASSESSMENT TOOL

Do you agree or disagree with these statements?

1. I appreciate other people's advice at work.
2. It's not my job to applaud others' achievements.
3. People lose respect when they admit their limitations.
4. I am entitled to more respect than the average person.
5. I do many things better than almost everyone I know.
6. It annoys me when others ignore my accomplishments.

Take a minute to consider them.

According to Hogan, people high in humility tend to agree with Item 1 and disagree with Items 2 through 6.[27] So, tell us: how'd you do?

Who's Using the Skill Well

We've defined humility. We've tied it to business storytelling. We've made the business case. We've shown you some ways to build the skill. Now, let's see who's using the skill well in business. We'll look at two brands from two different business sectors. One is a regional beer company, and one is a global outdoor-clothing retailer. Each has become a beloved brand in its own space.

Narragansett, Rhode Island is on the Northeastern seaboard of the U.S. and is known primarily for its beautiful beaches and coastline. But Narragansett is also the name of a longstanding regional beer. Narragansett beer was founded in 1890. It dominated the New England beer market for a good part of the twentieth century. In fact, it owned two-thirds of that market from 1919 to 1967. To put that into perspective, they held that market share from the year of the Paris Peace Conference that ended World War I to the release of The Beatles' Sgt. Pepper's album.

By the 1980s, however, the brand—which had been bought out by another beer company in the mid-1960s—was a shell of its former self. But Mark Hellendrung, former CEO of Nantucket Nectars, and a group of Rhode Island investors saw something in Narragansett others didn't see. They saw a regional legacy brand with a storied past and the potential for a future. They bought the company in 2005.[28]

Would you believe that in the span of six years, production of Narragansett beer went from 6,000 cases a year to 600,000 cases a year?[29] No, we didn't accidentally type a couple of extra zeros. The year 2017 marked Narragansett's twelfth consecutive year of growth. They did $8 million in sales in the first half of 2017 alone.

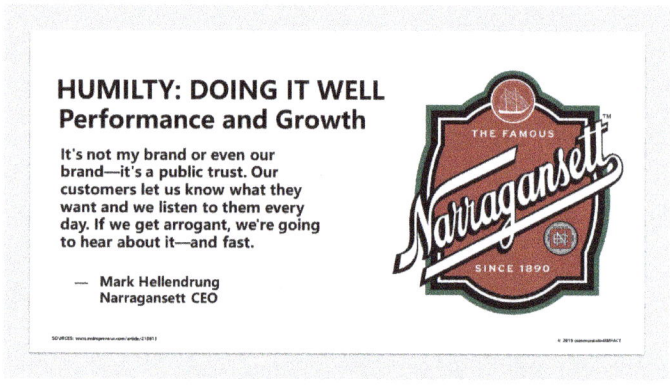

IMAGE SOURCE: narragansettbeer.com

Additionally, over the past year, the brewery grew 21 percent. And it has plans to build a new facility in 2020.[30] But perhaps most emblematic of Narragansett's success is that the beer is being sold again at Fenway Park, home of the Boston Red Sox, after having been pushed out for years by a larger global brand.[31]

To say that a lot went into this incredible turnaround is an understatement. But in our view, one of the key foundational factors underpinning this success story is the mindset of humility.

Here's how Hellendrung views the company he leads: "It's not my brand or even our brand—it's a public trust," he says. "Our customers let us know what they want and we listen to them every day. If we get arrogant, we're going to hear about it—and fast."[32] Clearly, humility is at the core of Narragansett's business and allows the company to prioritize its customers above everything else.

Next, we'll consider Patagonia. Patagonia—the place—is home to breathtaking, majestic beauty. It's also the inspiration and namesake for one of the world's leading retailers.

IMAGE SOURCE: Google Search

An article in *The Wall Street Journal* detailed how humility permeates Patagonia's culture. The article talked about how hiring managers are known for asking receptionists how they were treated by prospective hires. Dean Carter, Patagonia's global head of HR, will ask receptionists, "How did they [interviewees] engage at the front desk?"[33]

Testing for humility, even just anecdotally, is on Carter's radar as well as Patagonia's. Carter goes on to say that "humble employees are also more likely to support the company's mission of helping solve environmental problems."[34] Now that's looking at the big picture by looking toward the future.

We've looked at two companies who are doing humility well. Now, we'll close out our chapter with a discussion of something called humbition. As you have no doubt guessed, humbition combines humility and ambition—two words that you normally wouldn't put together. It's a term cited in a Bill Taylor piece entitled, *If Humility Is So Important, Why Are Leaders So Arrogant?*

Bill Taylor is not only a noted author—he's one of the co-founders of the business publication, *Fast Company*. Here's how Taylor frames this idea of humbition: "humility in the service of ambition is the most effective and sustainable mindset for leaders who aspire to do big things in a world filled with huge unknowns."[35] (There's that word "unknown," again.)

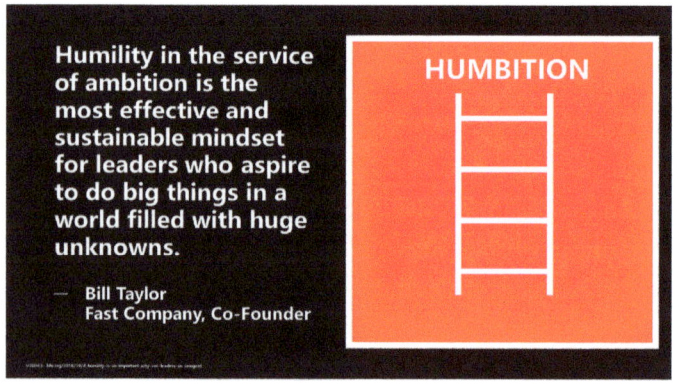

IMAGE SOURCE: Pixabay

As Taylor points out in the piece, the term *humbition* was first coined by a group in human resources at IBM.[36] Here's how they explained the origins of the term: "We noticed that by far the lion's share of world-changing luminaries are humble people. These world-changing luminaries share some common aspects. They focus on the work, not themselves. They seek success—they are ambitious—but they are humbled when it arrives. They feel lucky, not all-powerful."[37]

As we think about it, it occurs to us that if *humbition* had a tagline (not that it needs one) it might be this gem from Sir Isaac Newton: "If I have seen further, it is by standing upon the shoulders of giants."[38]

RECAP

- Humility isn't thinking less of yourself; it's thinking of yourself less.
- Humility correlates to job performance.
- Humility is essential for learning.
- Be humbitious.

CHAPTER TWO
EMPATHY

People will try to convince you that you should keep empathy out of your career. Don't accept this false premise.

—**Tim Cook,**
Apple CEO, *MIT Commencement Address*[39]

Define the Quality

Now, LET'S MOVE on to the second of our five human qualities, the cousin of humility: empathy. What's the first thing you think of when you hear the word empathy? Understanding how someone else is feeling? Putting yourself in someone else's shoes? Seeing things from another person's perspective?

Here's a dictionary definition: "The quality that allows you to understand and share another person's feelings and emotions."

But this book is about winning with decency for better business, so how exactly does understanding and sharing the feelings of another help drive your bottom line or make for a better customer experience?

For our purposes, we'll look at the role of empathy in business along the lines of Microsoft CEO Satya Nadella. Nadella sees empathy this way. He says, "My passion is to put empathy at the center of everything I pursue—from the products we launch, to the new markets we enter, to the employees, customers and partners we work with." [40]

IMAGE SOURCE: Pixabay

Nadella understands that there are two levels of empathy in business. The first level of empathy is understanding your audience, their pain points, and their worldview. By audience, we mean any number of stakeholders—customers, consumers, your workforce, and more.

The second level of empathy is having such a good sense of your audience from a position of understanding that you're able to anticipate their unexpressed needs. Empathy is key in understanding where your customer or audience is and where they might be heading.

Another CEO who believes in the role of empathy in business is Apple CEO Tim Cook. In fact, he feels so strongly about the role of empathy, he issued this call to action in an MIT commencement address: "People will try to convince you that you should keep empathy out of your career. Don't accept this false premise."[41]

Tie It to Business Storytelling

We've provided a definition of empathy and looked at its role in business. Now, let's tie it to business storytelling. To do that, we'll apply the "Once Upon A Time" storytelling structure used by Pixar, which has given the world of animation *Toy Story*, *Finding Nemo*, and more. For our purposes, we're going to use this structure in a business context.[42]

Take a moment to look at this arc. Where do you think empathy comes into play? In the beginning, in the middle, or in the end?

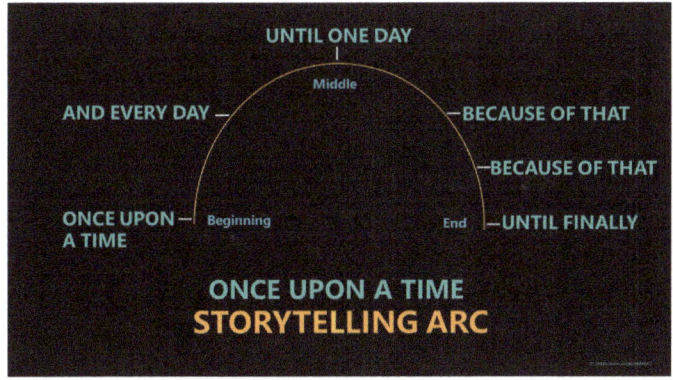

IMAGE CREDIT: Hatcher

Empathy comes into play at the very start with "Once Upon A Time," which establishes the current state—the ways things are for your customer, consumer, employee, or stakeholder. Empathy also comes into play at "And Every Day," where you learn about the problem or the pain points being experienced by your customer.

That same empathy helps form the basis for your product or service that comes in at "Until One Day," where you ultimately provide a solution. Are you surprised that the same story structure used to create your kid's favorite flick can be used in your business?

Make the Business Case

We've defined empathy. We've tied it to business storytelling. We've even begun to make some of the business case with the Pixar example. Now, let's take the business case a step further.

Remember when we talked about the boatload of dividends of winning with decency? Here's a big one. Research shows that empathy can boost your bottom line. A 2019 study published by *Businessolver* found that 90 percent of CEOs said they believe empathy is directly linked to a company's financial performance.[43]

Going back a few years prior, a 2016 Empathy Index published by *Harvard Business Review* (HBR) found a direct correlation between a company's empathy and its growth, productivity, and earnings. HBR measured companies' empathy through ethics, leadership, company culture, brand perception, and public messaging through social media.[44] Researchers found that the top 10 most empathetic companies increased in value more than twice as much as the bottom 10 and generated 50 percent more earnings.

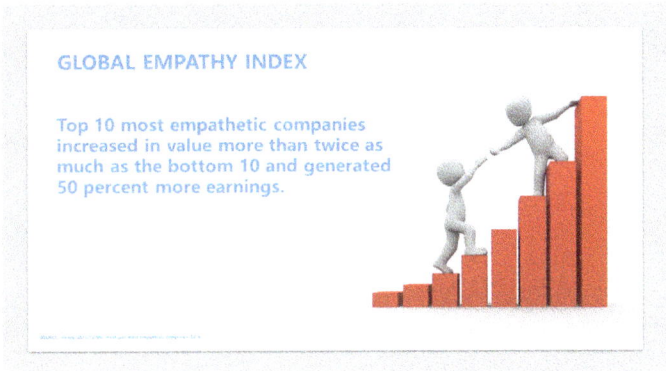

IMAGE SOURCE: Pixabay

Those companies included brands like Alphabet, Southwest Airlines, and Whole Foods. That same study also found that 93 percent of employees said they're more likely to stay with an empathetic employer.

Equally important, 87 percent of millennials said they would consider leaving an employer who they didn't think was empathetic enough.[45] Already, we see some of the dividends of decency as it pertains to empathy: higher earnings, better productivity, and stronger employee retention.

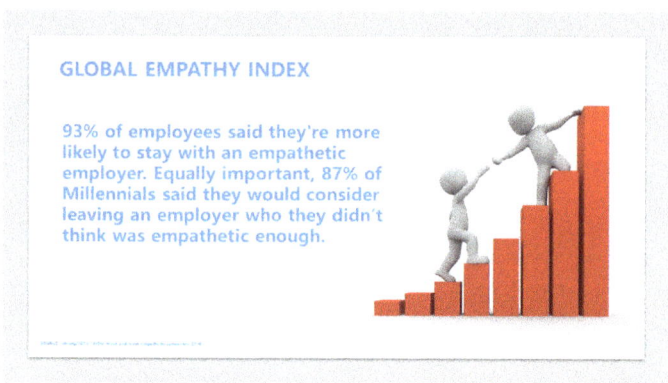

IMAGE SOURCE: Pixabay

The same article mentions Ryanair, which used empathy to transform its customer service. In 2014, Ryanair launched a customer-focused campaign called "Always Getting Better." The airline reduced its carry-on luggage restrictions and eliminated many hidden charges. Those—and other customer-focused changes—cumulatively resulted in a rise of 13 places in the 2016 Global Empathy Index. The campaign also resulted in a net profit increase from €867 million Euros the previous year to €1.24 billion Euros in the year ending March 2016.

This Ryanair example demonstrates the role empathy can play in driving your business, especially when it comes to customer service.

But to put a *Win With Decency* lens on it, we would propose taking the campaign a step further. We would change the word "getting" to "serving" in the campaign title. Why? Because "Always Getting Better" is about Ryanair. "Always Serving

Better" would be about its customers. A small change, but a distinction with a difference—one that solidifies the shift.

As we have demonstrated, empathy can play a huge role across your enterprise. Empathy is essential to protecting and growing your business. It drives everything from product development, user experience, and innovation to marketing, communications, and sales, as well as employee recruitment and retention. Again, a whole lot of decency dividends.

Transform the Quality into an Applicable Skill

We've defined empathy. We've tied it to business storytelling. We've made the business case. Now, let's transform the quality of empathy into an applicable skill. But to do that, you have to know how to listen. There are two kinds of listening: listening to respond and listening to understand. You don't want to listen to respond. Here's why.

Have you ever been in a conversation where you found yourself thinking about what you're going to say next, instead of really listening to the person you're talking with? Even more to the point—have you ever been in an argument with a spouse, partner, or colleague and found yourself forming your rebuttal as the other person is talking? This is called listening to respond, which isn't really listening at all. It's listening to rebut.

A more effective approach is something called listening to understand. This is an approach to listening that will help you build your empathy skills. It's about being in the moment, in the present—*being* present. How does this work in a business context like a sales call or a pitch?

Obviously, you want to know the points you plan to make. But you also want to know your pitch *so well* that you can empty your mind of your own thoughts to make room for the thoughts of the person you're interacting with. It's the act of listening to understand that helps you learn what your prospect needs. When that happens, you put yourself in a better position to close the sale.

We've talked about how to build the empathy skill by listening to understand. Now, let's take a look at how you can develop the empathy skill further through the following exercise. A former colleague used this ice breaker for one of his team retreats. He asked everyone seated at the conference table to take off their shoes. He asked them to take their pair of shoes and pass them to the person on their right. He then asked each person to try (as best they could without hurting themselves or the shoes) to put on the shoes and walk around. You get the idea. The point is to show what it feels like to walk in someone else's shoes—literally.

This kind of exercise is bound to produce more than a few chuckles and is an excellent way to get you and your team focused on empathy.

Using the Skill Well

We've defined empathy. We've tied it to business storytelling. We've made the business case. We've transformed the quality of empathy into the applicable skills of listening to respond and listening to understand. Now, let's see who's using the skill well.

First up is the eyewear company—Warby Parker. Check out the photo of the cleaning cloth that comes in their eyewear cases. Written on the cloth are several points of empathy in the hundred-word story of how Warby Parker was founded. How many can you find?

> **Warby Parker in 100 Words**
> Once upon a time, a young man left his glasses on an airplane. He tried to buy new glasses. But new glasses were expensive. "Why is it so hard to buy stylish glasses without spending a fortune on them?" he wondered. He returned to school and told his friends. "We should start a company to sell amazing glasses for non-insane prices," said one. "We should make shopping for glasses fun," said another. "We should distribute a pair of glasses to someone in need for every pair sold," said a third. Eureka! Warby Parker was born.

IMAGE CREDIT: Hatcher

We're sure you found them all, but just in case (no pun intended), here they are. Empathy Point #1: Almost everyone has lost a pair of glasses. Empathy Point #2: Replacing eyeglasses can really be expensive. Empathy Point #3: It's hard to find stylish eyeglasses that are affordable. Empathy Point #4: We all want to be seen as someone who helps someone else in need. Empathy, empathy, empathy. Warby Parker is doing empathy well.

Here's an example of how another company is creating empathy but by using artificial intelligence (AI). Yes, you read that right. The mattress company Casper created a free chatbot specifically for insomniacs. (Because at 3 a.m., who doesn't want to talk to a friendly ghost, right?) To use it, customers simply text "Insomnobot3000" and talk about whatever is on their minds, and Casper's bot will have real conversations with them.

With the Insomnobot3000, Casper is able to collect mobile numbers and send insomniacs promotional offers and discounts for their mattresses. And here's how something artificial turned into something real. Casper pulled in $100 million in sales its first year of launching the chatbot.[46] Decency dividend—check (literally).

This next company discovered the dividends of empathy after doing some homework. When Google wanted to find out what made for great teams, it launched an initiative in 2012 called "Project Aristotle." Hoping to find an algorithm that pointed to great team characteristics, it came up empty-handed. After input from sociologists and psychologists, Google found that great teams are made up of people exhibiting particular behavioral patterns or *group norms* that algorithms couldn't detect.

Over a two-year period, the project studied 180 Google teams, conducted 200-plus interviews, and analyzed over 250 different team attributes. Google found that the single-greatest attribute for a team's success was not intellect, experience, seniority, or educational pedigree. It was something called psychological safety—a group environment where members felt safe and free to share ideas or opinions without fear of judgment. The key to facilitating that safe environment was empathy.[47]

So, what are the dividends of empathy here? Breakthroughs that might not otherwise happen have a chance to see the light of day. Bad news that would otherwise go unspoken gets communicated.

Pulitzer-prize-winning reporter and author Charles Duhigg had this to say about Project Aristotle and its outcomes:

> The behaviors that create psychological safety—conversational turn-taking and empathy—are part of the same unwritten rules we often turn to, as individuals, when we need to establish a bond.
>
> And those human bonds matter as much at work as anywhere else. In fact, they sometimes matter more.[48]

As we have shown, empathy has played and is playing a key role across successful businesses. And we have to throw in one more example of a company that's doing empathy well. How are they doing it well? They are putting empathy right at the center of their culture. The company is Microsoft, and the number-one advocate and champion for empathy is none other than its CEO, Satya Nadella, who we quoted at the outset. But interestingly, Nadella has not always been the global ambassador for empathy.

Here's a story he likes to tell about himself. The source for this particular account was a fireside chat at the University of Nebraska.[49] When Nadella first interviewed at Microsoft, he did very well. No surprise there. He fielded and answered a battery of tough, technical questions. He didn't get tripped up once. But the final question was a different matter, and it threw him for a loop. The question was this: "If a baby falls down in a crosswalk just as the light turns green," the job interviewer asked, "what do you do?" Nadella thought for a second and then said… "I'd call 911."[50]

After hours of successfully answering questions, Nadella had finally given a wrong answer. His interviewer told the future Microsoft CEO, "You need some empathy" as they walked to the door. The interviewer's parting comment to Nadella was this: "When a baby falls, the first thing you do is pick the baby up and hug them."[51]

It's one thing to realize that empathy is important. It's another thing to internalize it and then integrate it into the very fabric of your enterprise. That's exactly what Nadella has done at Microsoft. Here's what one employee had to say on a Microsoft page dedicated to empathy and innovation: "[Satya Nadella] fosters this culture of learning and of respectfully questioning each other, to try to understand the other perspectives. The whole emphasis on empathy is really shining through in situations where there's a dire need to innovate and create something individuals need and want."[52]

This touches on empathy's role in innovation. Delivering on what people need and want is innovation gold. And Microsoft has its mouse (or touchpad) on the pulse of empathy when it comes to prototyping user experiences. When you begin product development with the user experience in mind, you have a much better chance of ensuring that—as one Microsoft principal said—"empathy is built *into* your product, not bolted on."[53]

For us, as trainers in business storytelling, we're all over this. It's long been our belief that product development should start with a story, not with a solution. Preferably, it's a story that begins with what your hero (your customer) wants and what's standing in their way from getting it. We sum up this approach by saying "begin with the end user."

Okay, but what has all of this empathy done for Microsoft? Open about his own journey and demonstrating the power of empathetic leadership, Nadella has moved his company's culture and business in an incredible direction. As a *Bloomberg* headline put it, Microsoft "has more subscribers than Netflix, more cloud computing revenue than Google, and a near-trillion-dollar market cap." As of April 2019, Microsoft's valuation has topped $1 trillion and is up more than 230 percent since Nadella became CEO five years ago. But he's challenging his company not to look to the past but to look to the future, which is exactly what he is doing with a culture that's bringing along the next generation of leaders in tech and business.[54] And, as if all that weren't enough, *Fortune* magazine named Nadella its Businessperson of the Year for 2019.

We realize that this chapter on empathy is one of the longest in the book. We've covered a lot. But empathy is the bedrock of making whatever it is you're selling matter in a way that will inspire action. In short, empathy is essential to using the *Win With Decency* strategy.

Now, we're going to wrap up this section, not with a business example, but with a riveting story of how empathy saved someone's life. This story is a powerful reminder that the qualities we're talking about in this book are *human* qualities, after all. These qualities are deeply rooted in the human psyche. Qualities that Abraham Lincoln captures for the ages in his use of "better angels" in his first inaugural address. In this story, those better angels were called upon—and they answered back.[55] This is how the story goes.

A twenty-something triathlete—Nathalie Birli—was cycling near her home in southern Austria when, out of nowhere, a man rammed his car into her, knocking her and her bike to the ground. That was bad enough. But he hit her on purpose.

And even that wasn't the worst of the story. The man then proceeded to abduct Nathalie Birli, bringing her back to his home, where he threatened to kill her. She was terrified. But as terrifying as the possibility of death was, nothing was as horrible to her as the thought of never seeing her newborn son again.

Yes, she was a triathlete and in top shape. But it wasn't her physical power that would ultimately save her. It was the unexpected power of empathy. Here's what happened to Nathalie Birli, as reported by *The New York Times*:

> In a moment of quiet, "when he was not beating or threatening me," she looked around, noticed the orchids and without thinking, commented on them. "I just threw it out there, that his orchids were so beautiful." She added that she had orchids as well and knew how much care went into keeping the delicate blooms alive and thriving."
>
> "Suddenly, he started talking about how he cared for them, using water from his aquarium," she said. "Suddenly, he was a completely different person."

This simple expression of empathy—manifested in a shared love of orchids—created the initial trust that Nathalie was able to build upon. She smartly used this opening—caused by empathy—to her advantage. This would eventually lead to her release. But once again, in a truth-is-stranger-than-fiction moment, would you believe that the kidnapper who rammed her with his car and threatened to kill her ended up driving her home? Once she got in her house, she locked the doors and called law enforcement, and her captor was arrested. Obviously, this is an extreme example, and a horrifying one at that. But it speaks to the ineffable power of empathy to foster human connection.

RECAP

- Empathy is central to innovation.
- Empathy helps you understand the pain points of your customer.
- There's evidence that empathetic companies see higher earnings.
- Empathy helps with talent retention.
- Empathy can create a psychologically safe environment for groups to share ideas.
- And yes, it might also save your life.

CHAPTER THREE
VULNERABILITY

Vulnerability is about building trust—the backbone of successful leadership.

— **Warren Buffett**

Define the Quality

WE'VE TALKED ABOUT the first two qualities of humility and empathy. Now, let's turn to vulnerability. What's the first thing you think of when you hear the word vulnerability? Weakness, liability, a threat, exposure to risk? Here's a dictionary definition—vulnerability is "the quality or condition of being easily hurt or attacked."

How can something associated with being easily hurt strengthen your business and your business leadership? Here's how Warren Buffett defines vulnerability: "vulnerability is about building trust—the backbone of successful leadership."

Considering Warren Buffett's definition and taking inspiration from Dr. Brené Brown—a world expert on vulnerability—we'll define vulnerability as follows. It's the exposure, the emotional tripwire you feel when you step outside your comfort zone. That emotional exposure creates a connection between you and your audience or customer. Vulnerability is an invitation. It creates:

- Trust
- Connection
- Leadership
- Executive Presence

All of which you need to retain talent, build your brand, manage your reputation, and grow your business.

Tie It to Business Storytelling

We've defined vulnerability. Now, let's see how it relates to business storytelling. Many companies make the mistake of being positive, positive, positive in their storytelling in a way that puts them in the best light possible. But something about that just doesn't feel right. Does anyone live a life that is positive, positive, positive, with no challenges, no obstacles, no downturns, no hitting rock bottom…ever?[56] Storytelling that's all positive is not relatable, credible, or authentic. It's just not how we live our lives.

IMAGE SOURCE: Canva

Think about it this way: who are you more likely to root for in a story? Someone who's living a life where everything is awesome? Or someone who's had to face a big obstacle and still found a way to overcome it?

Let's face it—more often than not, we root for the underdog. So, how do you use vulnerability in your business storytelling? This is how. You use struggle strategically. You use struggle to create common ground where your customer thinks, "Yeah, I've been there…" They're *nodding yes* instead of *nodding off*.

Because most organizations shy away or even run away from exposing their struggles, mastering the art of using struggle in a strategic way can be a huge competitive advantage. To show you what we mean, take a look at this ad. Is there anything or anyone to root for? Do you see yourself in this story?

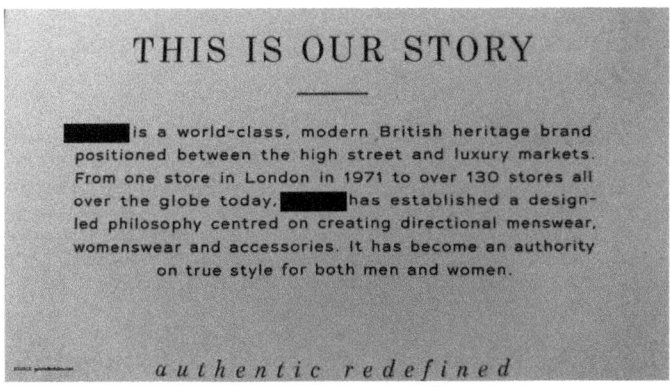

IMAGE SOURCE: gabrielledolan.com

Let's contrast this ad with the Warby Parker example we shared earlier. Read through it, again.

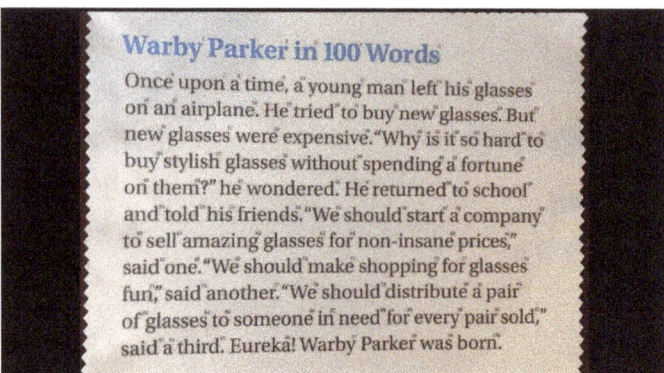

IMAGE CREDIT: Hatcher

Which one do you feel expresses vulnerability and uses struggle strategically? Which one makes you say, "Yeah, I've been there"?

By the way, here's a pair of Warby Parker sunglasses we purchased.

IMAGE CREDIT: Hatcher

And guess what? They even get the case right. Do you see where it says "nice to see you" on the inside? Almost every other brand you can think of would have a nice imprint of their brand's name. But not Warby Parker. Here's the message they're sending: They're not in business for themselves. They're in business to help consumers get amazing glasses at non-insane prices.

Make the Business Case

We've defined vulnerability. We've tied it to business storytelling. Now, let's make the business case. To do that, we'll examine some learnings from a *Harvard Business Review* article by professors Peter Fuda and Richard Bahdman, of Australia's Macquarie Graduate School of Management.[57]

In the article, they share some of their findings from a 2011 CEO study on what it takes to become a highly effective leader. The one key thread among the seven CEOs profiled wasn't what you might expect. It wasn't decisiveness. It wasn't vision. It wasn't strategic acumen. The common thread was the importance of vulnerability to effective leadership. We'll share two examples from the study.

Example #1

A managing director of a large beauty corporation was exasperated by a culture that lacked accountability. In his leadership team, he saw passivity, where he wanted to see initiative. Something had to give. But a funny thing happened on the way to blaming his team. After a 360-review of his own leadership style, he received feedback from his team that he was too directive—too one-way in management and communication.

He had a choice at that point. He could quietly work to rectify the situation behind closed doors, or he could take a different tack—a direction that would not only help him but his team and company as well. The first choice was safe and more conventional. The second was risky and would require vulnerability.

He opted for choice number two and decided to take accountability for his actions. He stood before top management at an annual meeting and publicly admitted his mistakes. He articulated a plan, not only for himself but for the organization. He was forthright in saying that he didn't have all of the answers, and he asked his team for help.[58] He used struggle strategically.

Here are some of the results. The organization saw a change in the managing director's communications style. One-way, directive communication evolved into open-ended questions that encouraged leadership from his team.

Let's take a moment and think about all of this. Is anything standing out for you here? None of this could have happened if the managing director had not been open to being a continuous learner. He could not have asked his team for help without humility, and he would not have taken accountability for his actions without vulnerability.

What were the dividends of decency in this story? Well, as the HBR article noted, "the managing director's effectiveness surged and his team flourished; dependent behaviors gave way to initiative and innovation, and his organization has outperformed much larger competitors in the six years since."[59]

Example #2

Here's a second story about a leader who had accepted a role as the CEO of a chemical and pharmaceutical multinational. Employee engagement was down. Financial performance was down. Initial change management efforts by the CEO weren't working. There was a culture of bullying that the CEO was trying to eliminate. But his own bullying conduct, according to the professors, was furthering a culture he was trying to change.

The CEO made a conscious effort to improve communications channels between his colleagues. Improved channels allowed for better feedback loops and increased self-awareness on the CEO's part. The culture shift that the CEO had wanted was beginning to happen. But as it was in the first story, that shift had to be led from the top with vulnerability. Acrimony and bullying tactics that were sapping engagement and financial performance gave way to conscious intentions to interact better and collaborate more.

Changes in communications, in interactions, and in culture helped drive what had previously been an elusive turnaround. And to harken back to humility, did you notice the importance of self-awareness?

What were the dividends of decency in this story? The company exceeded all financial targets, and a once-toxic culture was transformed into an enviable one—one that earned a prestigious *Hewitt Best Employers* award.[60]

Transform the Quality into an Applicable Skill

We've defined vulnerability. We've tied it to business storytelling. We've made the business case. Now, let's transform the quality of vulnerability into an applicable skill. But how exactly can you practice vulnerability?

Here's one of the first things you can do: remember that LEADERS STAND. This is a call to action learned from Matt McFadyen of the AIP Group, a leadership inspiration company. Matt's an amazing guy. He's a world-adventurer and explorer. He's also the youngest Australian to reach the North Pole. In his seminars, Matt typically begins with the powerful idea that leaders stand. Let's connect this idea to vulnerability.

IMAGE SOURCE: Unsplash

Picture this. You're at a large conference and there's time for a Q-and-A after the keynote. You have a question. You raise your hand and are called upon. The mic runner brings you the microphone. Do you stay seated and ask your question? Or do you stand? What if no one else is standing when they speak? What should you do? The answer is simple: leaders stand, even if it's uncomfortable.

Here's a real-world example. Our company conducted a series of business storytelling workshops in a country that is fast-becoming one of *the* tech hubs in Africa—Rwanda. One workshop took place in a bank boardroom with four CEOs and an official from the Central Bank of Rwanda. After sharing Matt McFadyen's mantra that leaders stand, each executive was asked to stand whenever they were called upon or wanted to speak.

The CEO whose boardroom we were using said she used to stand during meetings when she spoke, but had stopped doing so because others on the board weren't standing when they had something to say. She said that after the workshop, she was going to start standing again, regardless. Wow! *This* is why we do what we do. It gets better. She texted the organizer and said the workshop was "life changing."

Remember, if you've got something worth saying, it's worth standing up for, even if it makes you feel vulnerable. If you can't stand up for yourself, how can you stand up for anyone else? Leaders stand.

The second thing you can do to transform vulnerability into a skill involves social media. Get comfortable taking your followers behind the scenes in your posts. Reveal yourself to people, even when you think you're not at your best. Not in a way that's damaging to your reputation, professionally or personally, but in a way that's affirming of your humanity. In other words, share photos or video, even on bad hair days! Vulnerability = relatability.

Practicing vulnerability is not always easy to do! But it's one of those things where, the more you do it, the better and more comfortable you'll get at it. Not only will you and your message resonate better because you're more relatable, you'll also be far more productive when you're not focused on perfection.

Social media icon Gary Vaynerchuk offers some good advice on how to do this. When it comes to content, *document, don't create.*[61] Don't just show the finished product. Show what went into the finished product. This is how to gain customers, but more importantly, it's how you gain ambassadors and fans.

IMAGE SOURCE: Unsplash

So, what does *document, don't create* look like? Let's say you are going to be speaking to a large group and you're backstage getting ready. Have someone take a snapshot for a post on social media with a caption that says something like this: "Hey guys, getting ready to talk with all of you in about 90 min. Can't wait. Super pumped. #yourock."

Using the Skill Well

We've defined vulnerability. We've tied it to business storytelling. We've made the business case. We've transformed the quality of vulnerability into an applicable skill. Now, let's see who's using the skill well.

One example of a company using vulnerability well and weaving it within its culture is the insurance company John Hancock. Its CEO, Marianne Harrison—the first female CEO since the company's founding 157 years ago—is leading the way. We learned about her leadership efforts from a *Forbes* interview conducted by Rachel Montañez.

John Hancock has created an internal initiative fittingly called the John Hancock Signature Series. The series provides a platform for employees to share big ideas and personal experiences. The goal, according to Harrison, is "to address the stigma around vulnerability in the workplace and really try to encourage people to bring their whole selves to work."[62] From Hancock's website, we learned that an additional purpose of the series is to challenge the company's usual way of thinking and spark new conversations.

The John Hancock Signature Series provides a safe environment for vulnerability reminiscent of Project Aristotle's psychological safety outcome for empathy. In both cases, vulnerability and empathy foster open channels for freer, more authentic communications—essential for spurring innovations as well as anticipating blind spots or disruption. If empathy is fundamental to building a safe environment for dialogue, vulnerability is what allows you to participate in those conversations and contribute to them in a meaningful way.

John Hancock is one example of a company doing vulnerability well. The company in our next example is not one we would typically associate with vulnerability. And yet, it has kind of "corporatized" vulnerability by creating a culture where failure is not only tolerated—it's expected in order to progress and to innovate. The company is Amazon, and the example comes from Jeff Bezos' 2018 Shareholder Letter:

> As a company grows, everything needs to scale, including the size of your failed experiments. If the size of your failures isn't growing, you're not going to be inventing at a size that can actually move the needle. Amazon will be experimenting at the right scale for a company of our size if we occasionally have multi-billion-dollar failures. Of course, we won't undertake such experiments cavalierly. We will work hard to make them good bets.[63]

Here you have one of the top CEOs on the planet giving his workforce not only the permission to fail, but the expectation of failing…at scale. It's also an incredibly astute way of managing the expectations, not only of his shareholders but of Wall Street analysts and reporters. He's saying, in effect, *we're building failure into our business model—get used to it.*

Vulnerability is the ultimate bridge to connecting with your audience, customer, or workforce in a way that builds trust, connection, leadership, and executive presence. Done well, vulnerability humanizes a leader and a company, drives innovation, eyes potential disruption, and allows for a fail-fast culture.

RECAP

- Vulnerability is the exposure—the emotional trip wire—you feel when you step outside your comfort zone.
- To practice vulnerability, remember that leaders stand.
- Vulnerability connects and builds trust.
- Vulnerability has the courage to be wrong and the wisdom to see failure as a rung on the ladder of success.
- Vulnerability takes your audience behind the scenes.

CHAPTER FOUR
GRATITUDE

Gratitude is happiness doubled by wonder.

—**G. K. Chesterton**

Making the extra effort to say thanks in a genuine, personal manner goes a long way.[64]

—**Sir Richard Branson**

Define the Quality

WE'VE TALKED ABOUT humility, empathy, and vulnerability. Now, let's turn to our fourth quality: gratitude. What comes to your mind when you hear the word gratitude? Probably things like being appreciative or not taking things for granted. Here's a dictionary definition of gratitude: "the quality of being grateful or thankful."

For our purposes, we'll think of gratitude in two ways. There's **experiencing gratitude** and then there's **expressing gratitude**. British author G.K. Chesterton speaks to the *experience* of gratitude when he writes that "gratitude is happiness doubled by wonder."

Sir Richard Branson speaks to the *expression* of gratitude when he says that "making the extra effort to say thanks in a genuine, personal manner goes a long way."[65] In this chapter, we'll show you how both forms of gratitude play a key role in business.

Tie It to Business Storytelling

We've defined gratitude in two ways. Now, let's tie it to business storytelling. First, we'll use an example of experiencing gratitude.

Experiencing Gratitude

One of the benefits of *experiencing* gratitude is the ability to notice and appreciate small details—a benefit that allows you to add greater specificity to your business storytelling. Specificity adds context to your communications, keeps you from being too generic, and makes what you're saying relatable. Advertising icon David Ogilvy demonstrated the power of experiencing gratitude in an iconic ad for Rolls-Royce in 1959.

In doing his research for the ad, Ogilvy spent three weeks learning everything he could about the new model. Part of this research included riding in the car. Ogilvy noticed how incredibly quiet the ride was, even at higher speeds. When writing the ad copy, Ogilvy could have simply made note of the quiet.

Instead, he used specificity and wrote: "at 60 miles an hour the loudest noise in this new Rolls-Royce comes from the electric clock."

Ogilvy's experience of gratitude for the quiet ride equipped and sensitized him to notice small details. It allowed him to be captivated by the quiet. It was so quiet all he could hear was the clock. These details allowed him to paint a specific picture that was relatable.[66]

Like the consumers his ad was designed to reach, Ogilvy experienced a certain happiness derived from a smooth, quiet ride, and that happiness was indeed doubled by wonder when he realized that all he could hear was the clock's ticking.

"At 60 miles an hour the loudest noise in this new Rolls-Royce comes from the electric clock"

IMAGE SOURCE: March 1959 Ad created by David Ogilvy

Expressing Gratitude

We've talked about experiencing gratitude as it pertains to business storytelling. Now, we'll move to expressing gratitude. We'll do that while keeping in mind Sir Richard Branson's point that "making the extra effort to say thanks in a genuine, personal manner goes a long way."[67] One of the benefits of expressing gratitude is the connection it creates between you and your audience—it's a connection that says, "You have changed me for the better." And one of the most important parts of storytelling is transformation.

Here's an example of someone expressing gratitude that Lisa-Marie experienced as an audience member. Award-winning actress and singer Kristin Chenoweth returned to Broadway in November 2019 for a limited-run engagement called, *For the Girls*. The show was, in essence, a love-letter from Chenoweth to her favorite female recording artists.

IMAGE CREDIT: Hatcher

In contrast to the stage for *Wicked* (where Chenoweth had knocked the audience's socks off by portraying Glinda, almost two decades prior) a bare floor with a backdrop of soft lighting and a few musicians served as the setting.

Evocative of a teenage girl's slumber party, the opening scene had Chenoweth walking out on stage in an oversized white tee-shirt. She then sat on the floor as she went through a pile of her favorite record albums. The audience had been invited into her sacred space and began to reminisce with her.

Moments later, Chenoweth was crooning tunes from the likes of Barbra Streisand, Judy Garland, Linda Ronstadt, Patsy Cline, Karen Carpenter, and more. Shared between songs were words of gratitude from Chenoweth on how these women had shaped her life through youth, love and loss, and mentorship with their music.

While saying thank you to her beloved artists for the ways their music had impacted and inspired her, Chenoweth was also saying thank you to her audience by sharing her amazing voice in such an intimate and personal way.

But the real highlight was at the end of the show, when Chenoweth sang Dolly Parton's, *I Will Always Love You*. The song was a love letter to Dolly, but Chenoweth turned it into a love letter of gratitude for her fans. On the last verse, she returned the microphone back to its stand, while the musicians stopped playing and the lights dimmed. Chenoweth walked to the edge of the stage and sang the last verse acapella.

And for a few moments, between Chenoweth's sung words, this 1,200-seat, full-to-capacity crowd at The Nederlander Theater on Broadway was spellbound in adoring silence. Here's what Ben Brantley, co-chief theater critic for *The New York Times*, had to say: "And when, as a finale, Chenoweth tossed aside the microphone to deliver a heartbroken rendition of *I Will Always Love You* by Dolly Parton, I found tears in my eyes for the first time that night."[68]

Chenoweth expressed gratitude, and her audience experienced it. The sweet spot for gratitude in business storytelling happens when a brand makes the extra effort to say thanks in a genuine and personal way that creates not just happiness, but happiness that is doubled by wonder. When this occurs, both parties are changed for the better.

Now that we've wiped our eyes and cleared our throats, let's make the business case for gratitude. We believe that, done well, gratitude has the greatest untapped ROI potential in business.

Why? Because gratitude helps drive the two things that businesses need most to survive and thrive: **employee loyalty** and **customer loyalty**.

Employee Loyalty

Let's start with employee loyalty and look at the numbers. According to a Hays Recruiting report, 71 percent of today's workforce would consider leaving their job for the right offer.[69] Even at top Silicon Valley firms like Apple and Google, employees on average leave after two years or less.[70]

Tech Tenure
The Average Number of Years at Tech Disruptors and Titans

● Tech Disruptors ● Titans

Facebook	2.02
Google	1.90
Oracle	1.89
Apple	1.85
Amazon	1.84
Twitter	1.83
Microsoft	1.81
Airbnb	1.64
Snap Inc.	1.62
Uber	1.23

Note | Tech Titans are public companies with an IPO over 10 years ago and a current valuation of over $100 billion. Tech Disruptors are privately held companies or public companies with an IPO in the last 10 years and a current valuation of over $10 billion.

Source | Paysa

What's going on here? What's driving this turnover trend? Low pay? Actually, research shows it's not about the money. In fact, 71 percent of employees would willingly take a pay cut for an ideal job.[71]

Turnover is largely attributed to employee disengagement, stemming from a lack of appreciation. According to the employee recognition firm Achievers, 90 percent of employees hope to be recognized at least once per quarter.[72] Apparently, this isn't happening.

Employee turnover has gotten so out of hand and the labor market has gotten so tight that a phenomenon associated with dating—called "ghosting"—is now applicable to the workplace. What is employer ghosting? Well, The Federal Reserve Bank of Chicago, of all places, defines it this way: when a worker stops coming to work without notice and then is impossible to contact.[73] *The Washington Post* even ran a story with the headline: "Workers are ghosting their employers like bad dates."[74]

This new culture of employer ghosting must be met with a culture of employer gratitude. Employers must invest in worker appreciation with the same level of commitment as other investments in their business. This means saying thank you to your employees consistently and genuinely for a job well done. But don't stop there—thank your employees for contributions, too, some of which cannot be quantified. For example, by all means, thank an employee for exceeding their sales target by 25 percent. But also, make sure to thank an employee who has mentored a group of new hires.

Customer Loyalty

We've talked about employee loyalty. Now, let's look at customer loyalty. Customer loyalty is more important than ever. A 2019 Forbes contributor article cited a study of 34,000 consumers worldwide that "showed customer loyalty and retention are declining." The article goes on to say that "two-thirds surveyed said they would be more likely to switch to a competitor that provided better customer service or a better overall experience." [75]

Just as it's not about salary for employees to be loyal, it's not just about price point for customers to be loyal. Employees want to be appreciated. Customers want to be appreciated. We speak from personal experience. Check out the postcard we received after joining the community of a U.K. content marketing firm called Atomic.

Gratitude   65

Now, here's the note on the back of the postcard.

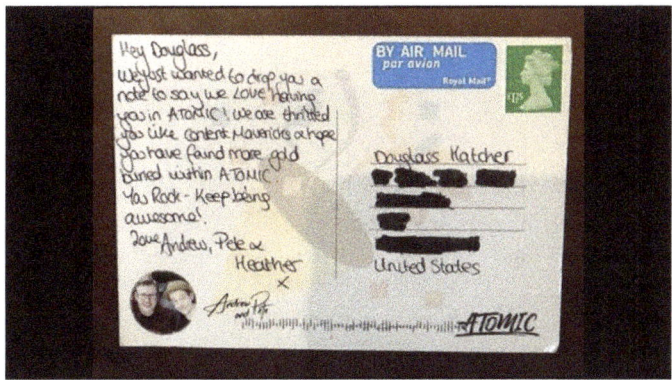

As you can see, it's a handwritten thank you note from the founders of the company—Andrew and Pete—as well as Heather, our point of contact. We kept the card. We shared it on social media. We blogged about it. We shared the love.

There are plenty of competitors in Atomic's space. But it's this expression of gratitude in the form of a handwritten thank you note that made us feel like valued customers and in turn, made them stand out. At a time when technology affords greater opportunities to target and segment consumers, this is what personal looks like in personalization.

Transform the Quality into an Applicable Skill

We've defined gratitude in two ways—experienced and expressed—and tied them both to business storytelling. We've made the business case that gratitude drives employee loyalty and customer loyalty. Now, let's transform the quality of gratitude into an applicable skill that drives those loyalties—first for employees and then for customers.

Gratitude as a Skill for Employee Loyalty

When you think of the practice of gratitude, there's probably nothing as ubiquitous as the "gratitude journal," where you get in the habit of writing down some things you're grateful for. But have you thought about creating a gratitude journal, not for yourself, but for your employees?

Let's say you have a team of ten direct reports. At the beginning of each quarter, buy ten journals. Label each journal with the direct report's name. At the end of each day, take a moment to write down something in each person's journal that they did that you're grateful for. At the end of the quarter, each journal will have a list of up to sixty expressions of gratitude from you. Gift wrap each journal and give them to your direct reports. This will show them in a tangible way that you noticed the little things along the way and that you made it a daily practice to recognize their contributions to you and the team. In a world where employee loyalty is increasingly fleeting, a little gratitude from you can go a long way.

Gratitude as a Skill for Customer Loyalty

Now, let's look at one way you can apply gratitude as a skill in gaining customer loyalty. This involves social media listening and monitoring to look for opportunities to express gratitude to your customers. Here's an example from a sippy cup company, Tommee Tippee cups. On their Twitter feed, the company came across a father who needed to replace a limited-edition sippy cup for his autistic son, Ben. This cup was the only one Ben would use, but it was disintegrating. In a desperate attempt to replace the cup, the father created a hashtag campaign called #cupforBen and the tweet went viral. Because Tommee Tippee was using social media listening and monitoring its Twitter feed, it was able to learn about the problem and do something about it.

IMAGE SOURCE: @OrigGrumpyDad

How did Tommee Tippee respond? They announced they would create a limited run of 500 of the discontinued cups, especially for Ben. That's how to turn listening into a memorable customer service experience and show an expression of gratitude for customer loyalty.[76]

Tommee Tippee said thank you in a very big way. But of course, there are little ways of saying thanks that can make a difference to both customers and employees over time. For example, if a customer or employee follows you on Twitter or Instagram, return the follow. If you see an opportunity on LinkedIn to endorse a customer or an employee, make the endorsement. All these things add up. They are the pavers on the pathway to loyalty.

Who's Using the Skill Well

Now, let's see who else is using the skill of gratitude well when it comes to employees and customers.

Using the Skill of Gratitude Well with Employees

Our first example comes from Sheldon Yellen, CEO of the disaster-relief, property-restoration company, BELFOR Holdings, Inc. Every year, Yellen hand-writes birthday cards to each of his 9,200 employees as a form of appreciation. He has been doing this since 1985, long before he became CEO. He also writes handwritten thank you and anniversary notes and recognizes other special occasions.

"It's also something that doesn't have to cost a thing," he said. "When I learn of random acts of kindness being performed in the field, I take it upon myself to again, reach out in writing, and send a thank you card so that person can know they are appreciated and that their efforts don't go unnoticed."

How can this expression of gratitude *not* impact employee morale, performance and loyalty? Yellen himself said that his gesture made for a more compassionate, gracious workplace. Gratitude is contagious. In fact, other managers at Yellen's company have even taken up the habit of writing cards for their team members, clients, and loved ones.

While some CEOs may consider the gesture of hand-written notes a time waster, Yellen is quick to disagree. "When leaders forget about the human element, they're holding back their companies and limiting the success of others," he said. "Focusing only on profit and forgetting that a company's most important asset is its people will ultimately stifle a company's growth." [77]

Another example comes from Doug Conant, former CEO of Campbell's Soup. When Conant became president and CEO in 2001, Campbell's Soup was facing significant market and financial headwinds. Things weren't much better internally. According to a *Fast Company* article, employee morale was low, teams were dysfunctional, and trust was lacking. In Conant's words, it was a "very toxic culture." Conant recognized that "you can't expect a company to perform at high levels unless people are personally engaged" and set out to change this. During an 11-year period, Conant sent over 30,000 handwritten notes of appreciation to employees for their contributions—from maintenance people to senior executives.

As a result, by 2009, the company experienced a complete turnaround.[78] Campbell's Soup outperformed both the S&P Food Group and the S&P 500. Sales and earnings were up, and so was employee morale. In fact, the company had 17 people who were enthusiastically engaged for every 1 employee who wasn't.[79] This was a sea-change from 2001 when for every two people actively engaged, one person was looking for a job.

Gratitude   71

IMAGE SOURCE: Pixabay

By actively recognizing employees at every level with small gestures of appreciation, Conant was able to transform a culture of toxicity into a culture of gratitude and success.

We've reviewed two great examples of how demonstrating gratitude toward employees can make a difference. Now, let's look at how an organization is doing gratitude well when it comes to its *customers*.

Using the Skill of Gratitude Well with Customers

The Baltimore Orioles are a storied major league franchise with a great tradition of winning. But the team has struggled in the last few seasons. An organization that has produced a number of Hall of Famers (including Cal Ripken, Jr.) had the second-worst record in Major League Baseball in 2019. This was only a slight improvement over the prior season when they had the worst record in baseball. Oriole Park at Camden Yards, one of the most fan-friendly ballparks in the country, was nearly two-thirds empty for most of the 2019 season.

Understandably, the Orioles could have begun their off-season focused solely on themselves and improvements for the next year. But that's not what they did. The players and the organization decided to thank their fans instead, after getting onboard with an idea brought to them by PR Director Kristen Hudak.[80]

Hudak suggested that a number of season-ticket holders should be randomly selected to receive a hand-written thank you note from one of thirty players. Here's an excerpt from one of the notes as reported by *The Washington Post*:[81]

IMAGE SOURCE: *The Washington Post*

"I'm sure some games were tough for you as a fan, but things will be back to the way they were soon enough!" third baseman Rio Ruiz wrote in his message to a fan named Ron. "Hope to see more of you in the next coming seasons. Many blessings!"[82]

While the Orioles did not make it to the World Series in 2019, they surely made it to the World Series of Gratitude.

As we've just seen, the positive multiplier effect of gratitude comes in various shapes and sizes. We'll close out this section with an example of how gratitude helps you persist in the midst of tough times. The example we'll use comes from an article in *Runner's World*.

The author of the article wanted to discover some tips and tricks for getting through those tougher moments on a run when you're ready to quit. She put out a call for tips on Instagram. One of the most popular tips that came back was this idea of something called the Gratitude Mile—where a runner will use a mile to think about what they are thankful for in order to shift their mindset from one of "I can't go on" to "I've come too far to quit now."

The article quotes Melissa Emery, who kicked off the Instagram response with the following:

> "THE GRATITUDE MILE! Once I hit a wall, I spend the next mile focusing on the things I am grateful for. 'I am grateful for this beautiful view, I am grateful for the sidewalk, I am grateful for the sun, I am grateful for my legs, and even though they hurt, I know I can do this, etc.' By the time the mile ends, the wall has been lifted and I continue on."

The article continues with this quote from a follow up interview with Emery: "It's easy to focus too much on pace, times, and chasing the next PR (personal record). The Gratitude Mile helps you find yourself again and appreciate the fact that you are able to run at all," says Emery. "I begin by simply taking notice and appreciating the simple things along my run."[83] Check out the word "notice" and think back to how David Ogilvy was able to infuse specificity in his iconic Rolls Royce ad.

Gratitude reminds us that counting your blessings can really count, whether it's appreciating your direct reports, colleagues, or fans, or just trying to push through a tough stretch of running in a race.

RECAP

- The experience of gratitude helps you notice and appreciate small details—a benefit that allows you to add greater specificity to your business storytelling, which keeps you from being too generic and makes what you're communicating more relatable.
- Gratitude helps drive the two things that most businesses need to survive and thrive: *employee* loyalty and *customer* loyalty.
- The cost of gratitude is small compared to its potential ROI.
- Gratitude helps you persist, which in a business context is essential for entrepreneurs and start-ups.

CHAPTER FIVE
GENEROSITY

Giving customers more than they expected. This is the generosity approach. [84]

— **Jay Baer**

WE'VE SHARED A lot of great examples so far about how the qualities of humility, empathy, vulnerability, and gratitude can be converted into skills for winning with decency for better business. And now, we've reached our fifth and final quality: generosity. What's the first thing that comes to your mind when you hear the word generosity? Probably words like giving, sharing, unselfishness, benevolence, or charitableness. Here's a dictionary definition of generosity: "the quality of being willing to share."

For our purposes, we'll define generosity along the lines of social media influencer, Jay Baer, who says it's, "giving customers more than they expected. This is the generosity approach."

Simple, right? But does generosity mean giving away the store?

IMAGE SOURCE: Pixabay

No, it doesn't. But by giving customers more than they expect, you can create a gateway to building deeper, stronger relationships, which leads to greater customer loyalty and higher profits. That's the ROI over the long-term. That's how you profit from the *Win With Decency* dividends.

Tie It to Business Storytelling

We've defined generosity. Now, let's tie it to business storytelling. Generosity in business storytelling prioritizes the experience of the audience you want to reach. Remember what we said about business storytelling in our chapter on humility? Your audience could be a customer, a reporter, a boss, a direct report—anyone you want to influence.

Generosity in business storytelling happens anytime you make the extra effort to ensure that what you're trying to get across is relatable, relevant, and meaningful to your audience. The smartest, most effective way of demonstrating generosity in business storytelling is to "give your customer the cape"—make your customer the hero.

We alluded to this in the humility section, where we said to make your business not about you but about your customer. We took this idea a step further in the vulnerability section, where we talked about using struggle strategically. When you give your customer the cape, you're offering a product or service that not only solves an important problem but transforms their life for the better. You help make them the hero of their own story.

Transformation in storytelling has long been the mainstay of great advertising. In today's marketplace, there is a University of Phoenix ad that does this beautifully. The 2019 "Discover Your Wings" TV spot shows a hardworking mom who longs for a better future for herself and her son. She discovers the University of Phoenix and enrolls in online courses. She pursues a degree with lots of late-night studying. She graduates from school and into the life she always wanted. She's the hero. Her "cape" was educational opportunity on her terms.

IMAGE SOURCE: Pexels

To be clear, we are referring to this one University of Phoenix campaign for illustrative purposes only. We are not referring to ad campaigns of the past or the future.

Make the Business Case

We've defined generosity, we've tied it to business storytelling… now, let's make the business case. Generosity in business can take the form of CSR (Corporate Social Responsibility) as well as philanthropy. Both have their place. But there is another way to show generosity in business, and that is by providing a sample of your product for free.

A sample can mean many things, depending on what type of business you are in. It could be a free consultation. It could be an e-book highlighting key takeaways from your workshop. It could be a blogpost that offers up some solutions to your consumers' problems. Your free content can be almost anything, but it must be of value to your customer. Free content that's valuable can accomplish many things, from building a fan base to building your credibility in a certain space.

Here's a fictitious but relatable example: Let's say you have a new ice cream brand. You're ready to introduce your product to the marketplace. You've gotten lucky and secured a prime spot at your local grocery store to distribute samples.

As the miniature cups filled with goodness are "scooped up," people are raving about your product. You've gone from no one knowing your name to becoming a real, bona fide, legit, credible maker of ice cream.

Not only that, you've just increased your chances of selling a few containers, because people now know that they *love* your ice-cream. As an added bonus, you've just started a word-of-mouth marketing campaign surrounding the deliciousness of your product. And to top it all off with a cherry on top, people will spend a little more money on your brand of ice cream than your competitor's just because they met you in person.

Now here's a real-world example of how generosity can set up a new business for success. Mint.com—an online financial management tool—used free content to promote brand awareness and credibility *before* they launched. They published their free content in the form of a personal finance blog called MintLife. This ramp-up garnered great results. By the time Mint.com was ready to launch, it had already engaged an audience of more than twenty thousand people via MintLife. Mint.com was eventually sold to Intuit for $170 million. And yes, you could say they made a "mint."[85]

Transform the Quality into an Applicable Skill

We've defined generosity, we've tied it to business storytelling, and we've made the business case. Now, let's transform the quality of generosity into an applicable skill.

IMAGE SOURCE: Pixabay

Here's one approach we found in a *Fast Company* article written by Wharton School professor, Adam Grant.[86] It's a group exercise called *The Reciprocity Ring*, which Professor Grant first learned about from University of Michigan sociologist Wayne Baker and social scientist Cheryl Baker.[87] Its purpose, in part, is to foster information-sharing to help solve problems in real time. Each participant makes a request to their fellow team members. Those teammates then combine their collective expertise in order to match solutions to requests.

Here are two examples cited by Professor Grant. In the first example, a pharmaceutical executive needed to synthesize a drug and wanted to keep the cost under the $50,000 price quoted by a vendor. Through *The Reciprocity Ring*, the executive found a colleague who had the expertise and lab capacity to synthesize the drug for free. In the second example, a Wharton student of Professor Grant's had always wanted to work at the amusement park Six Flags. But Six Flags didn't recruit at Wharton. Through *The Reciprocity Ring*, the student landed an introduction to a former Six Flags CEO.[88]

Creating a culture of generosity can have a multiplier effect in your business. Potential benefits include fewer silos, less information-hoarding, better communication, greater team collaboration, and overall improved productivity.

Who's Doing It Well

We defined generosity. We've tied it to business storytelling. We've made the business case and we've looked at some ways to build the skill. Now, let's see who's making generosity part of their business—let's see who's doing generosity well.

We'll take a look at three brands, representing three different business sectors. The first is in the clothing retail space. The second is in the entertainment streaming space. The third is in the food space.

Let's start with the giant online shoe retailer Zappos. Their CEO, Tony Hsieh, tells the following moving story;[89] A woman had been shopping for her husband in search of a particular brand of shoe. Unsuccessful in her search, she almost gave up. Finally, she found the shoes on Zappos and ordered them. But before the shoes arrived, her husband was tragically killed in a car accident. Wanting to return the shoes, the grief-stricken wife called Zappos. The call center employee who received her request did his job and promptly processed the return. But the story doesn't end there.

The call center employee then took the initiative to send flowers to the customer's home, expressing condolences on behalf of Zappos. While you're not likely to find specific guidance for this situation in the Zappos employee handbook, what you will find at Zappos is a culture of generosity.

As promised, here's our second example, which comes from a leader in the entertainment streaming space—Netflix. Generosity helped drive growth several years ago when Netflix was really coming into its own. This example has to do with the Netflix release of the series *House of Cards* back in February 2013. As Eddie Yoon points out in a *Harvard Business Review* article, Netflix decided to release all thirteen episodes at once. Today, this is standard practice, but it wasn't six years ago.

CEO Reed Hastings justified the move, saying that it "reinforced our brand attribute of giving customers complete control over how and when they enjoy entertainment."[90] But Wall Street wasn't so sure. There was a concern that some consumers would take advantage of Netflix's free one-month trial, proceed to watch all thirteen *House of Cards* episodes, and then not renew their subscription. But fewer than eight thousand people actually did this— or equivalent to 0.6 percent of the 1.3 million people who signed on for the free trial. Eddie Yoon captures this outcome with the following equation: Value = Benefits > Price > Costs.[91]

The third and final example of a company that's doing generosity well comes from the food space. It's yogurt-maker Chobani. But first, a little history from Chobani founder,

Hamdi Ulukaya.[92] For him, yogurt has always been personal. He grew up in Turkey, eating his mother's yogurt, which she made from scratch on their dairy farm. When he arrived in the U.S. in 1994, he was unable to find a comparable yogurt product. He started making his own at home, using his mother's recipe.

Around this same time, Ulukaya owned a feta cheese company called Euphrates. Because it was barely breaking even, he was primed for a new business opportunity. In 2005, he stumbled across a junk mail ad (yes – true!) selling an old yogurt factory in upstate New York. It was a fully equipped facility owned by Kraft Foods, which had decided to get out of the yogurt business.

Thanks in large part to a U.S. Small Business Administration loan, Ulukaya seized the moment and bought the facility. He hired a master yogurt-maker from Turkey, and together they perfected his mother's recipe.

After two years of revamping the facility and fine-tuning the product, Ulukaya was ready to go to market. But in a U.S. marketplace unfamiliar with Greek yogurt, he had to fight for two things. He had to fight for distribution in mainstream grocery stores, and he had to fight for shelf space in the dairy aisle alongside traditional yogurt brands. Ulukaya knew that if his product was only sold in specialty stores or in specialty aisles, he wouldn't be able to scale as quickly. His persistence paid off, not only for him, but for many Chobani employees as well.[93] Scaling quickly allowed him to keep Chobani privately held, without the use of equity investors.

This is all a backdrop to an announcement Ulukaya made a few years ago that he was giving a portion of his company to his employees. These so-called "Chobani Shares" were worth up to 10 percent of the company and could be transferred to stock or cash in the event of going public or being offered up for sale.

It's one thing to give equity in a start-up or in the early life of a company, but in this case, Chobani's valuation had increased to somewhere between $3 and $5 billion. For a company of around two thousand employees, a 10-percent payout would average around $150K.[94] Ulukaya recognized that he hadn't built his company by himself.

Generosity as a competitive advantage begins by giving more to your consumers than they expect and more to your employees than they expect. All three of these examples from Zappos, Netflix, and Chobani share a common generosity trait. To take a cue from noted author and professor, Carol Dweck, these examples reflect a growth mindset as opposed to a fixed mindset.[95] Generosity conditions us to operate, not out of scarcity, but out of abundance.

The opposite of generosity isn't stinginess, it's desperation. Desperation reaches out to get—generosity reaches out to give. Guess what? Your customers can sense desperation and generosity in equal measure.

Desperation pushes them away—generosity pulls them in. In fact, generosity creates a perfect storm of gratitude and confidence that can lead to the trust you need to forge a great relationship.

Generosity

The opposite of generosity isn't stinginess. It's desperation. Desperation reaches out to get. Generosity reaches out to give.

IMAGE SOURCE: Pixabay

RECAP

- Give your customer the cape. Make them the hero.
- Give away free, valuable content to increase brand awareness and credibility.
- Generosity can have a powerful multiplier effect, driving growth and scale.
- Generosity conditions us to operate not out of scarcity, but out of abundance.

CHAPTER SIX
KEEP THE HUMAN IN HUMAN ENTERPRISE

The wonders of the world are many, but none—none is more wondrous than Man.

— **Sophocles**, *Antigone*

THE WONDERS AT the time of Ancient Greece that Sophocles pondered were indeed great. Many of those wonders are still here for us to reflect upon today, and many new ones have evolved. But there are wonders to come that we can't even imagine, especially when it comes to technology and its impact on business. While the landscape of how we live and work is changing faster than ever, Sophocles reminds us that through it all, humankind remains the most wondrous.

In the 2020s, when skills will be depreciating faster than ever and traditional preparation for business will no longer be enough, we will all need to draw from the well of human resources. While it has its place, we are not talking about the department down the hall. We are talking about the human resources of humility, empathy, vulnerability, gratitude, and generosity. These are resources that have been with us for thousands of years—that remain at the ready to position you for success and winning with decency.

We must remember that the greatest competitive advantage in business isn't our technology, but rather our humanity. Maximizing that advantage comes down to one simple call to action: keep the human in human enterprise.

Winning With Decency starts with you. But in case you're wondering how much of an impact you can make by implementing this strategy, there's now research that quantifies your chances of making a difference. During rigorous testing within an online community that used incentives to motivate actions, researchers from the University of Pennsylvania and the University of London found that the tipping point for social change within a group is 25 percent.

If you can get 25 percent of your group, organization, or company on board with a change, there's a good chance the entire group will adopt that change—which makes what could be daunting, doable.[96]

It's been said that the future isn't what it used to be. While that feels truer than ever, we believe that—with your help, your leadership, and a strategy to *Win With Decency*—the future will not only be different, it will be better.

ABOUT THE AUTHORS

Douglass and Lisa-Marie Hatcher are co-founders of communicate4IMPACT (C4I), a marketing and communications firm that specializes in business storytelling training. Douglass previously led thought leadership and executive communications at Mastercard in Purchase, New York. Prior to Mastercard, Douglass spent two decades in Washington, DC, where he worked on Capitol Hill in senior positions in both the U.S. Senate and House. Lisa-Marie's background is in account development and sales. She has worked in the public sector at the U.S. Department of Defense as well as in the private sector in both pharmaceutical sales and global finance. The couple resides in Westchester County, New York, where they are raising their twins.

ENDNOTES

1. http://www.twainquotes.com/Right.html

Introduction

2. http://www.abrahamlincolnonline.org/lincoln/speeches/congress.htm
3. https://www.smartcitiesworld.net/news/news/5g-predicted-to-generate-17-trillion-by-2035-starting-with-cities-4258
4. https://fs.blog/2018/03/half-life/
5. https://www.ibm.com/downloads/cas/EPYMNBJA
6. https://bigthink.com/philip-perry/47-of-jobs-in-the-next-25-years-will-disappear-according-to-oxford-university
7. https://www.huffingtonpost.ca/entry/85-of-jobs-that-will-exist-in-2030-haven-t-been-invented-yet-d_ca_5cd4e7dae4b07bc72973112c
8. https://hrexecutive.com/now-is-the-time-to-start-upskilling-your-workforce/
9. https://www.nato.int/docu/speech/2002/s020606g.htm

Chapter One—Humility

10 Rick Warren, *The Purpose-Driven Life*, (Zondervan and Rick Warren, 2002, 2011, 2012, 2018), e-book, Kindle Edition, P. 5.

11 https://www.dictionary.com/browse/humility

12 Rick Warren, *The Purpose-Driven Life*.

13 Carmine Gallo. *Talk Like Ted* (St. Martin's Press, 2014).

14 Daniel H. Pink *To Sell Is Human: The Surprising Truth About Moving Others*, (Penguin Publishing Group, 2012), e-book, Kindle Edition, P. 70.

15 Bradley P. Owens, Michael D. Johnson, Terence R. Mitchell, "Expressed Humility in Organizations: Implications for Performance, Teams, and Leadership," *Organization Science* 24, no. 5 (2013): 1517-1538.

16 https://www.brookings.edu/opinions/adam-smith-preached-self-interest-and-self-help-too/

17 https://www.theguardian.com/sustainable-business/unilver-ceo-paul-polman-purpose-profits

18 https://www.fastcompany.com/90419047/how-empathy-became-the-new-ceo-status-symbol

19 Bradley P. Owens, Michael D. Johnson, Terence R. Mitchell, "Expressed Humility in Organizations: Implications for Performance, Teams, and Leadership," *Organization Science* 24, no. 5 (2013): 1517-1538.

20 https://www.wsj.com/articles/why-investors-might-want-to-bet-on-humble-ceos-11572836641

21 https://onlinelibrary.wiley.com/doi/abs/10.1002/smj.3071?af=R

22 https://www.businessinsider.com/satya-nadella-microsoft-ceo-qa-2017-4

23 https://www.cnbc.com/2017/05/25/nio-ceo-padmasree-warrior-3-traits-you-need-to-succeed-in-tech.html

24 https://news.stanford.edu/2005/06/14/jobs-061505/

25 https://www.marketwatch.com/story/%20serena-williams-says-its-really-important-to-learn-this-skill----and-how-you-can-kill-it-at-work-by-learning-new-things-too-2018-12-10

26 https://bcghendersoninstitute.com/winning-the-20s-the-new-logic-of-competition-7c1500c5a187

27 https://www.wsj.com/articles/the-best-bosses-are-humble-bosses-1539092123

28 https://www.entrepreneur.com/article/219613

29 Ibid.

30 https://www.barrons.com/articles/how-passion-investors-helped-revive-narragansett-beer-1506130542

31 Ibid.

32 https://www.entrepreneur.com/article/219613

33 https://www.wsj.com/articles/why-investors-might-want-to-bet-on-humble-ceos-11572836641

34 https://on.wsj.com/2k8toIC

35 https://www.hbr.org/2018/10/if-humility-is-so-important-why-are-leaders-so-arrogant

36 Ibid.

37 Ibid.

Chapter Two—Empathy

38 Isaac Newton letter to Robert Hooke, February 5, 1675 (Historical Society of Pennsylvania)

39 https://qz.com/1002570/watch-live-apple-ceo-tim-cook-delivers-mits-2017-commencement-speech/

40 https://twentyonetoys.com/blogs/future-of-work/3-ceos-using-empathy-to-unlock-innovation

41 https://qz.com/1002570/watch-live-apple-ceo-tim-cook-delivers-mits-2017-commencement-speech/

42 Daniel H. Pink, *To Sell Is Human: The Surprising Truth About Moving Others*, (Penguin Publishing Group, 2012), e-book, Kindle edition, P. 70.

43 https://blog.businessolver.com/the-2019-state-of-workplace-empathy-study-the-competitive-edge-leaders-are-missing

44 https://hbr.org/2016/12/the-most-and-least-empathetic-companies-2016

45 Ibid.

46 https://senseimarketing.com/10-unique-customer-experience-examples-best-practices-boost-brand/

47 https://www.inc.com/michael-schneider/google-thought-they-knew-how-to-create-the-perfect.html

48 https://www.nytimes.com/2016/02/28/magazine/what-google-learned-from-its-quest-to-build-the-perfect-team.html

49 https://journalstar.com/news/local/education/microsoft-ceo-in-lincoln-empathy-paves-the-way-for-innovation/article_0e8dcf1a-6056-5fe0-af87-a87640dcaf7c.html

50 Ibid.

51 Ibid.

52 https://news.microsoft.com/innovation-stories/empathy-innovation-accessibility/

53 https://medium.com/microsoft-design/prototyping-empathy-1bdb08e3260c

54 https://www.bloomberg.com/news/features/2019-05-02/satya-nadella-remade-microsoft-as-world-s-most-valuable-company

55 https://www.nytimes.com/2019/07/30/world/europe/austria-cyclist-abducted.html

Chapter Three—Vulnerability

56 Robert McKee, Storynomics lecture, 2017, New York, NY.

57 https://hbr.org/2011/11/fire-snowball-mask-movie-how-leaders-spark-and-sustain-change

58 Ibid.

59 Ibid.

60 Ibid.

61 https://www.garyvaynerchuk.com/creating-content-that-builds-your-personal-brand

62 https://www.forbes.com/sites/rachelmontanez/2019/10/14/

how-one-leading-financial-firm-is-creating-a-culture-of-vulnerability/#4f1551aa726d

Chapter Four—Gratitude

63 https://blog.aboutamazon.com/company-news/2018-letter-to-shareholders

64 https://www.virgin.com/richard-branson/why-we-should-all-send-more-thank-you-letters

65 Ibid.

66 http://rollsroyce-ogilvy.blogspot.com/

67 https://www.virgin.com/richard-branson/why-we-should-all-send-more-thank-you-letters

68 https://www.nytimes.com/2019/11/10/theater/kristin-chenoweth-broadway-ian-mckellen.html

69 https://www.hays.com/press-releases/us-workers-willing-to-compromise-on-salary-for-the-right-benefits-company-culture-and-career-growth-opportunities-2030744

70 https://www.forbes.com/sites/falonfatemi/2019/10/21/3-steps-to-prevent-employee-turnover/#79ff05ad6d9c

71 https://www.hays.com/press-releases/us-workers-willing-to-compromise-on-salary-for-the-right-benefits-company-culture-and-career-growth-opportunities-2030744

72 https://resources.achievers.com/resources/the-power-of-employee-appreciation/

73 https://www.washingtonpost.com/business/2018/12/12/workers-are-ghosting-their-employers-like-bad-dates/?arc404=true

74 Ibid.

75 https://www.forbes.com/sites/shephyken/2019/10/13/customer-loyalty-and-retention-are-in-decline/

76 https://www.tommeetippee.us/cupforben

77 https://www.businessinsider.com/ceo-writes-7400-employee-birthday-cards-each-year-2017-6

78 www.fastcompany.com/3035830/how-campbells-soups-former-ceo-turned-the-company-around

79 Ibid.

80 https://www.washingtonpost.com/sports/2019/10/04/orioles-players-thank-fans-with-handwritten-notes-after-another-brutal-season/

81 Ibid.

82 Ibid.

83 https://www.runnersworld.com/training/a29321193/gratitude-tips-for-long-run/

Chapter Five—*Generosity*

84 Jay Baer, *Talk Triggers* (Penguin Publishing Group, 2018), e-book, Kindle Edition P. 104.

85 https://www.inc.com/sonia-thompson/generosity-the-new-way-to-build-a-multi-million-dollar-business.html

86 https://www.fastcompany.com/40545869/adam-grant-can-help-you-coax-generosity-out-of-your-grumpiest-coworker

87 https://giveandtakeinc.com/reciprocity-ring/

88 https://www.fastcompany.com/40545869/

adam-grant-can-help-you-coax-generosity-out-of-your-grumpiest-coworker

89 Gideon F. For-mukwai, *The Science of Story Selling: How Win the Hearts & Minds of Your Prospects for Profit and Purpose* (Gideon F. For-mukwai, 2015), e-book, Kindle locations 566-574.

90 https://hbr.org/2013/05/netflix-reported-another-great

91 Ibid.

92 https://hbr.org/2013/10/chobanis-founder-on-growing-a-start-up-without-outside-investors

93 Ibid.

94 www.fastcompany.com/3059437/the-business-strategy-to-being-generous-to-employees

Chapter Six—Keep the Human in Human Enterprise

95 Carol Dweck, *Mindset: The Psychology of Success* (Random House Publishing Group, 2006, 2016), e-book, Kindle Edition.

96 https://futurism.com/social-change-tipping-point